QUIPNOTES
ABOUT MOMS

by
Barbara Birenbaum

PEARTREE®

Published by
PEARTREE®
P.O. Box 14533
Clearwater, Florida 33766-4533
USA

Copyright 2003
ISBN: 0935343-075

Printed in the United States of America
10 9 8 7 6 5 4 3 2 1

CIP Data
Birenbaum, Barbara
    Quipnotes about moms / by Barbara Birenbaum
    p.cm.
    1. Mothers—Quotations, maxims, etc.
    2. Motherhood—Quotations, maxims, etc.
    3. Mothers—Anecdotes. I. Title

PN6084.M6 B57 2003   00-053083
818'.5402—dc21

Contents

Introduction

Moms are called by many names—Mother, Ma, Mama, Mammy, Mum, Mommy and Mom. No matter what name is given to a Mom, each one is special around the world.

*Dedicated to my Mother and to my
children who made me a Mom*

These quips are dedicated to all the
Moms of the world who join together with
insight and understandings that only
Moms could perceive.

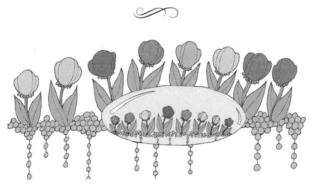

About Moms . . .

$\mathcal{M}$oms are gems,
so rare they can't
be mined!

Moms can't be traded
in because they
are priceless!

*M*oms are a special breed
that can't be found in
a pet store.

*M*oms may not
have everything,
but give 150% of what
they have.

*M*oms are patient,
just waiting for the
rewards of their efforts.

Moms take life
with a grain of humor.

*M*oms have a
built in sixth sense,
plus more in reserve.

*M*oms spend
a lifetime
experiencing children.

*M*oms bring balance
to the highs and lows
of living.

Moms have a wealth
of experience just
waiting to be tapped.

*M*oms love is everywhere,
even when it's out of sight.

$\mathcal{M}$oms learn
sign language when
children are born.

*M*oms insist that
mistakes are just
experiences of life.

*M*oms stretch dollars
like giraffes stretch
their necks.

*M*oms cuddle little
bundles that grow up
to be big surprises.

*M*oms watch
their little offspring
sprout into individuals.

$\mathcal{A}$dvice from Moms . . .

If you listen,
you might hear;
but if you hear,
will you listen?

If you see yourself
acting like Mom,
better check
your mirror.

If you mind your
p's and q's,
the other letters will
fall in line.

If you wait for
something to happen,
nothing gets accomplished.

If life throws you a curve,
figure out how to steer
around it.

If you are up
against a wall,
it keeps you out of a corner.

If you feel shut out
from the crowd,
open another door.

If you think
you can outsmart Mom,
try someone else.

If you take
stock in yourself,
your options grow.

If manners matter,
wear them at all times.

If your Mom is out,
she may be
making a delivery.

If you don't want advice,
    expect it anyhow.

If you run out of time,
it's only waiting
to be found.

If you learn something
new every day,
your mind gets energized.

If you cultivate a garden of friendships, living will be enriched.

If you wonder
about life,
it is waiting to be
discovered.

Moms seem to know . . .

*I*t's not hard to find a Mom. Just do or say something unexpected and she's there!

Children may want
to be left alone,
but like Moms to be
there in emergencies.

*M*oms know how
to make ends meet with
no strings attached.

$\mathcal{M}$oms toss life lines
to children in need.

*W*hen you don't like what
your Mom has to say,
where were you when she
said, "I told you so?"

*M*oms seem to know
what you mean when you
have little to say.

*M*oms make room
for children who want
their space.

*M*oms seem to know
how to steer children in
the right direction.

*M*oms offer
encouragement to
children who harbor
doubts.

$\mathcal{M}$oms look out for children who are trying to find themselves.

*M*oms sense when
children are hurting,
even when they don't cry!

*M*oms seem to know
more than children think
they know.

*M*oms rise in stature
once children grow up.

Moms to children . . .

*M*oms and children
may not see eye to eye,
but it pays to look, anyhow!

*W*ho would you be if you didn't have a Mom?

If you want only
positive input,
expect only half a charge
out of life!

If Mom caused
your problems,
how come you knew about
them first?

If Mom's cooking
was so bad,
how did you survive
to adulthood?

If you think you've
outgrown your home,
how come you enjoy
coming back?

You know Mom is
upset when your room
can stay a mess.

If Mom tries your
patience, there
must be a reason why.

If all Moms are alike,
what makes you think
you'll be any different?

What's cooking with Moms . . .

Moms are like pots of coffee, always brewing about something.

Moms are as refreshing as cups of brisk tea.

*M*oms season
food for thought
by caring.

$\mathcal{M}$oms who savor
life enjoy
their children.

*M*oms are like
microwave ovens,
getting heated up with
touches of energy.

*M*oms are good cooks,
able to make
a lot from a little.

*M*oms adorn the
table of life
with their presence.

$\mathcal{M}$oms dine on
the pleasures given
by children.

*M*oms feed children
balanced meals to
sustain them until they
stand on their own.

*M*oms nurture children
who fend for
themselves as adults.

*M*oms add the
ingredient of love
to whatever they make.

*M*oms who stay
out of the kitchen,
may get feedback
from children anyway.

$\mathcal{M}$oms love
can't be measured
because each
recipe is special.

*M*oms are creative cooks, turning recipes into original concoctions.

*M*oms find children
the dessert of life,
while enjoying other
courses of living.

*M*oms recipes for survival
include hearts filled with love,
measures of enthusiasm, dashes of
energy, blended with an endless
amount of patience,
seasoned with children's needs.

L*ogic from Moms . . .*

*M*oms find
value in children
who often underestimate
their worth.

*T*hose who
look down on Moms,
need to grow up.

$\mathcal{F}$ace it,
who came first,
Moms or children?

*M*oms see through
the illogic of
children's logic.

$\mathcal{M}$oms learn from
children what they
have yet to understand.

$\mathcal{M}$om is one
step ahead of you and
two steps behind.

If you can hug a pet,
you can hug
your Mom.

Seek your potential,
since only you
can find it!

*N*ourish your ideas
in the landscape
of creativity.

*U*nearth your talents
in the garden
of experience.

$\mathcal{B}$elieve in yourself
to cultivate
self-confidence.

Stretch for your dreams,
no matter how
way-out they seem.

*G*o after your goals,
but keep
a steady course.

*S*trike a balance
between your strengths
and limitations.

$\mathcal{H}$elp others feel good
about themselves.

*K*eep life in focus
with a clear
image of yourself.

*S*ize up your options
and take stock
in your decisions.

*M*arket yourself
in a well-rounded package.

If you paint a rosy picture, make sure the canvas has all the colors.

*S*elfhood comes
from living.

*A*rguments get you
nowhere with Moms
who have their
own agenda.

$\mathcal{F}$riends may come
and go,
but Moms are forever.

*W*ho says . . .

*Y*ou were never
there for me!
*Were you playing
hide-and-seek?*

*W*here were you when
I needed you?
*Trying to find out
what you needed!*

*P*lease be someone
else's Mom for a day!
*Fortunately, Moms can't
be given away.*

I want only
positive input.
*Then you'll get half
the charge of living.*

No one loves me.
Have you ever asked?

*W*hen can I have my say?
*When others are
willing to listen.*

Once is enough!
Are you testing the limits?

*S*top while you are ahead.
*How could Mom
know what direction
you're going?*

*L*iving takes a lifetime.
*Just wait around to see
if it's true.*

*M*om's life is easy.
*Tell me when
you are a parent.*

Why must you always
say that?
Because Mom cares.

*L*eave me alone.
*Moms would if they could,
but can't, so they won't!*

*S*top nagging me.
The word was omitted from
Mom's vocabulary.

I can do what I want.
So would Mom
if she had the time.

*G*et a life, Mom.
Sounds great!
Vacation starts tomorrow.

$\mathcal{W}hat\ if\dots$

If you can send e-mails,
then you can
write thank you notes.

If you come first
all the time,
you must live alone.

If rules were meant
to be broken,
they'd come with glue.

If you are taller than Mom, clean everything above her height.

If you are tall enough to
reach the sink,
help with the dishes.

If you ask, "Why?"
the answer must be, "No!"

If you ask,
"How come?" be prepared
to look up the answer!

If you can sit for hours
at the computer,
you can sit long enough
to do homework!

If you think Mom
is "bent out of shape,"
how come she is so
physically fit?

If you think Mom
is slowing down,
try keeping up with
her in a mall.

If you try a Mom's
patience,
she might try yours!

If you take pride in accomplishments, there must be a reason why.

If you call a Mom
by any other name,
it must be someone else.

Thank and ask Mom . . .

Whenever you are served your favorite meals, thank Mom.

*W*henever you think
you know it all,
ask Mom.

*W*henever your home
seems like a haven,
thank Mom.

*W*henever you want
an honest opinion,
ask Mom.

Whenever you use your manners, thank Mom.

Whenever you lose your bearings, ask Mom.

$\mathcal{W}$henever you
feel secure,
thank Mom.

*W*henever you
wonder who you are,
ask Mom.

Whenever you get your way, thank Mom.

Whenever you need reassurance, ask Mom.

Whenever your needs are met, thank Mom.

*W*hen all else fails,
ask Mom.
That's why she's Mom.

*H*elpful hints from Moms . . .

If you think you know it all, how come Mom's questions get no response?

*T*ake life in long strides
to overcome hurdles.

*L*earning
from mistakes changes
them to experiences.

*S*ometimes Moms could
walk away from it all,
but family ties get
in the way.

*"T*his is your Mother,"
means
Mom is really mad.

"*I*'ve had it,"
means
you are grounded!

*I*t's a Mom's right
to give many answers to
the same question.

$\mathcal{M}$oms are good people to start lives with.

*M*oms are always learning because they are home-schooled.

If you want to keep a pet, make sure your Mom likes it.

*T*hink before you act,
and you will act
as you would think.

If you have an image of
the person you want to be,
make sure it
includes yourself.

*M*oms make little
astronauts that soar
through life.

Just when . . .

*J*ust when Moms seem to
run low on energy,
they get wound up again.

*J*ust when Moms seem
to have lost their style,
they cultivate another.

*J*ust when Moms seem
out of sync,
they e-mail messages.

*J*ust when Moms seem to
lose their touch,
they surf the Internet.

*J*ust when you think
Moms no longer listen,
they hear with the
acuity of CD's.

*J*ust when you think
Moms have lost their cool,
they are having
hot flashes.

167

*J*ust when Moms like
you as you are,
you change before
their eyes.

*J*ust when Moms need hugs, they give them for no reason.

*J*ust when
Moms seem happy,
they cry.

*J*ust when
Moms seem to have
nothing to say,
they talk with their eyes.

$\mathcal{L}$*ovingly, Mom . . .*

*M*oms love is
measured by the
spoonfuls to be taken
over a lifetime.

*M*oms have feelings,
but it's hard to tell when
they are hurting.

*M*oms may
seek your love,
but will never say so.

*M*oms who
have wrinkles,
earned them.

*M*oms may not say so,
but need help
around the house!

*M*oms prefer
real communication to
phone messages
and e-mails.

*M*oms do puzzles
with children to figure
out how their lives
piece together.

*M*oms have a way of
laying cards on the table
when others don't even
know how to deal.

*M*oms play the game
of life with children
who think they have
already won it!

*M*oms sort through children's problems like laundry, but let them put their lives in order.

*M*oms realize
children grow up without
their permission.

*M*oms tell it like it is,
because they care.

*M*oms listen even
when children don't think
they can hear.

*M*oms bend over
backwards so children
can go forward
with their lives.

*M*oms have intrinsic
value that increases
with age.

Gifts for Moms . . .

*G*ive Mom some
peace of mind.

*T*ake the time to say,
"hello."

$\mathcal{T}$hank her for being
your Mom.

*G*ive Mom hugs when
least expected.

*W*hen in doubt,
buy flowers.

*H*elp Mom understand
how to work the DVD.

Show Mom shortcuts on the computer.

*P*encil in a day just
for Mom.

Share a recipe to make
meals special.

Take Mom out to lunch.

*I*nvite Mom to your home.

Nurture Mom's
love as she
has nurtured you.

Quipnotes about Moms . . .

*M*oms are like
flashlights,
turned on when you hope
they're turned off.

If you think
Moms can be replaced,
try shopping for one
in a mall.

If Mom has a word with you, it may be a discussion.

If you think on your feet,
it keeps you from
standing on your head.

If everything was child's play, there would be no school.

If you expect Mom to be there for you, better give her directions.

If you can dish it out,
plan on eating your words.

If you wait for Mom's
reaction,
get "call waiting."

$\mathcal{M}$oms are like
the Internet,
on line even if you're not.

*W*hen God made Moms . . .

*H*e knew
what he was doing.

*H*e didn't ask anyone
for permission.

*H*e felt she'd do
the best job.

$\mathcal{H}$e knew she was up
to the challenge.

*H*e had faith in
her ability.

*H*e knew she'd
find a way.

*H*e knew she's just
what children needed.

*H*e gave her
a permanent job.

*H*e gave her
a contract for life.

*H*e was proud of
his handiwork.

*H*e preserved the
mold for eternity.

*H*e blessed each
family with one.

*H*e made each Mom
different so children
could be unique.

Modern Moms . . .

*M*odern Moms
care enough to tell
children the way
things are.

Modern Moms
use a laptop and
a cell phone.

*M*odern Moms
communicate
by snail-mail, e-mail
and voice mail.

*M*odern Moms
can be counted on,
even if they can't
solve problems.

*M*odern Moms
stand in your corner,
when others have you
up against a wall.

Modern Moms
look ahead,
even when children
must toe the line.

*M*odern Moms
are known to be
good sports,
even if not athletic.

*M*odern Moms score points with children who are still learning to count.

*M*odern Moms
paint pretty pictures of
children who still
scribble with crayons.

*M*odern Moms
often use a mouse on a
mouse pad to get a
message across.

*M*odern Moms swapped
their phone book for
electronic organizers.

*M*odern Moms know
what it's like to be young,
even though children think
they were born old.

*M*odern Moms
have a lot of living to do
beyond parenting.

Tidbits and afterthoughts of Moms . . .

*M*oms who see things
as only black-and-white,
are colorblind when
it comes to children!

Moms who see things
in shades of gray,
use the other
colors to decorate!

*S*ome Moms work
at careers,
while others make
parenting their careers.

*S*ome Moms are
easy-going and care-free,
while others are
wrinkle-free.

$\mathcal{M}$oms lives are
in transit,
keeping up with children
in perpetual motion.

*I*t's often difficult
for Moms to keep quiet,
especially with noisy
children.

$\mathcal{M}$oms who take
back seats to children,
must be teaching them
how to drive.

$\mathcal{M}$oms brighten the
world like a rainbow.

*M*oms get to the
heart of a matter,
without missing a beat.

*M*oms know children
make a difference
in time and place.

Moms are forward
thinking when it comes
to thoughtfulness.

Moms ask for
nothing in return,
but reap the fulfillment
of parenthood.

*M*oms are what others can't be until they become one.

Moms who say
nothing, keep children
wondering why.

*I*t's a gift to be a
Mom because life is
a blessing.

*L*et's face it,
Moms are a difficult
act to follow.

Look for other titles
of this series
by Barbara Birenbaum

Quipnotes About Dads
Quipnotes About Aunts
Quipnotes About Uncles
Quipnotes About People

From PEARTREE®